Trust Yourself Anyway

How to Overcome Self Doubt, Quiet the Inner Critic, and Build Everyday Confidence Through Self Care and Honest Choices

Ellen M Bennet

Contents

Introduction — v

1. The Voice That Doubts You — 1
2. Where That Voice Came From — 9
3. The Cost of Letting It Lead Your Life — 17
4. Self Trust Is Not Confidence — 27
5. Turning the Critic into a Guide — 35
6. Small Acts of Courage Build Self Trust — 43
7. Let Yourself Be Seen Imperfectly — 52
8. A Life You Can Trust Yourself In — 58

A Note from the Author — 67

Introduction

There is a voice in your mind that tries to keep you safe. It comments on how you look, how you speak, how you work, who you love, and what you dream about. It points out every risk. It questions every decision.

> It treats mistakes
> like disasters.

It did not show up because something is wrong with you or it showed up because, at some point in your life, being careful felt necessary. Maybe you grew up trying not to upset anyone. Maybe you worked hard to be perfect, hoping someone would finally say you were enough…maybe you learned to keep your real thoughts quiet, so you would not be judged or rejected.

The voice learned its job in those moments. It decided that approval equals safety. It figured that if it could help you avoid mistakes, you would not lose love, respect, or belonging. It tried to protect you the only way it knew how.

Introduction

The problem is that you grew up.
The voice did not.

It still treats you like someone who needs permission before making a move.

It still believes fear is a warning, instead of a sign that you are doing something new. It still repeats rules that were useful once, but now only limit your life.

Many people try to silence this voice, they tell themselves to stop overthinking and try to act confident. They pretend they do not care and some try positive affirmations that feel fake. Others push themselves until they burn out.

This book does not take that approach. **We are not here to fight the voice.** We are here to understand it, then decide how much power it gets. You do not need to shut it down. You only need to stop letting it lead your life.

Think of this voice as a scared helper. It means well, but it does not know how to guide an adult life.

> Instead of letting it drive, you can learn to listen, take what is useful, and then make choices based on trust rather than fear.

In the chapters ahead, we will uncover where this voice came from, how it shapes your life today, and how you can respond to it with calm clarity instead of pressure or panic. You will learn to make choices that match who you are becoming, not who you were when the voice first formed.

Introduction

Along the way, I will share a few stories from my own life and from others who learned to build self trust one small choice at a time. Nothing dramatic, just moments that shaped how we think and who we believe we are allowed to be.

Each chapter will also offer simple tools. Not big transformations. Not miracle formulas. Just small practices you can actually use in ordinary life. A different way to talk to yourself. A new way to take a step. A quiet shift in how you treat your own thoughts.

If there is one promise this book makes, it is this:

you can learn to trust yourself, even while the inner critic still speaks.

Self trust does not mean you stop feeling afraid or making mistakes. It means you stop letting those things decide who you are allowed to be.

Let's begin.

Chapter 1
The Voice That Doubts You

You probably know the voice without needing anyone to describe it. It is the one that suddenly shows up when you want to say something honest, or try something new. It tells you to wait, to not embarrass yourself, to think a little more, to double check, to speak later, to stay quiet, to hold back. It sounds protective, but you can feel its pressure.

This chapter is not here to fight that voice. You will not be told to replace it with positive thinking or to pretend you feel brave when you do not. You will not be expected to act fearless or loud or bold. Instead, you will learn to look at the voice quietly, as if you are finally turning to see who has been whispering inside your head all these years.

> For now, we simply name the voice when it shows up. We notice it, instead of letting it take over.

This is the beginning of self trust.

You know the voice without needing to think about it

The inner critic does not always speak loudly. Sometimes it speaks so quietly that you do not hear words. You only feel something. A pause. A tightening. A thought that says not yet. Or maybe not at all.

Maybe you have an idea in your mind when you are in a conversation. You want to share it. It feels clear and simple. Your voice is ready to speak. Then, in a second, something inside tells you to wait. You think you need to organize your thoughts a little better, or find the right moment, or make sure your idea sounds smart.Instead of speaking, you hold it in. You nod. You listen. You say nothing.

Later, you think of the exact words you wanted to say, and you know they were not silly or useless. You were not confused or unprepared, you simply did not trust yourself enough to speak when the moment was real.

There is a feeling you recognize. A quiet heaviness in the body. Not shame, exactly. Not disappointment, exactly. Just a sense that something true was kept inside.

That is how the critic keeps you small without looking like an enemy. It does not attack you. It protects you so tightly that it stops you from being yourself.

A real moment of doubt

I will share a simple moment with you. Nothing dramatic. Just one of those times you remember for no clear reason, even though nothing tragic or important happened.

I was in a small conversation with two people. The topic was something I knew well. Not expert levels of knowing, but enough to speak clearly. The conversation was lively, friendly, relaxed. I understood the topic, I even had a perspective that could have helped the person who was confused. I was confident in other parts of life. I was not shy. Yet as I opened my mouth to contribute, something inside me tightened.

The thought was quiet. It said, in its own way, wait. Think more. You might be wrong. Someone else will explain it better. You will sound like you are trying too hard. They might not agree. You might make it awkward. Just listen instead.

I stayed quiet. I smiled. I nodded. I let someone else answer a question I could have helped with.

The moment passed like nothing. But the feeling stayed. Not humiliation. Not regret. Just a familiar sense of shrinking. I felt myself disappear a little, even while sitting right there with other people.

That is the moment the critic likes. Not the big ones. The small ones where you abandon your own voice without anyone noticing.

It is interesting how you can feel invisible while looking perfectly present.

What makes the critic speak?

The inner critic does not show up because you are weak. It does not speak because something is broken in your personality. It speaks because you were once shaped by moments where staying silent, being careful, or trying to impress others helped you fit in, stay safe, or avoid conflict.

Maybe as a child you learned not to upset anyone or you learned that others knew better. Perhaps you learned that being smart earned love, and being wrong risked losing it, or you learned that being agreeable protected you. Maybe you learned that attention was risky or that mistakes came with emotional consequences.

Whatever shaped the voice is old. You can feel its age. The tone feels outdated, like a set of rules you never agreed to as an adult, but still follow out of habit.

The voice believes it is keeping you safe. It thinks it is protecting your place in the world. It thinks speaking or expressing yourself is dangerous. Not physically dangerous, but socially dangerous. It believes that being misunderstood is a threat. That being judged is a threat. That being wrong means losing something important.

> It is a confused protector, doing its best, with rules it learned long ago.

How the critic shows up in everyday life

It does not only show up when you speak. It might show up in front of the mirror. You get dressed, and feel fine. You are ready for the day but then something inside picks apart your reflection. Too much of this... not enough of that. You leave the house, but the confidence inside you sinks a little.

It might show up when you try to rest. When you sit down to relax. The voice reminds you of unfinished tasks it questions whether you deserve rest. Rest becomes guilt instead of recovery.

It might show up when you try something creative. You have an idea. It feels exciting for a second, then the critic gives you reasons why it will not work, why no one will care, why someone else already did it better.

You step back, not because you are lazy, but because you do not want to feel foolish.

Or it might show up when someone compliments you. You want to simply receive the words. Instead, the critic argues with them in your mind. You push the compliment away as if the other person is mistaken.

You do not lack confidence. You lack permission from yourself.

That is the work of the critic.

The body reacts too

You might think the critic lives only in your mind, speaking in words or thoughts. But you can feel it in the body long before you hear the commentary.

There is a tightness in the chest, a shift in your breathing. Your shoulders tense. Your stomach tightens and your throat feels heavy. Your face might feel warm...not from shame, but from alertness.

The critic is not simply judging your thoughts. It is preparing you for imagined danger and sends warnings into your nervous system as if something terrible will happen if you express yourself or make a choice others might question.

The body reacts because the critic treats social risk as emotional danger.

It tries to protect you from rejection, embarrassment, failure, disappointment, or misunderstanding. It believes your safety in the world depends on how you are seen by others.

> It tries to help you survive moments that do not actually threaten you.

This is why noticing the critic is not only mental. You can feel it. You can sense the shift when it speaks.

Your thoughts pull back. Your body pulls back. Your voice pulls back.

We notice the voice without fighting it

When most people try to get rid of the critic, they end up reacting to it in ways that make it stronger. They tell themselves to stop overthinking, but the critic hears that and becomes even more alert. They try to hype themselves up, and the critic becomes suspicious, or they try to push through fear, and the critic becomes louder, insisting that something is wrong and they should wait.

Fighting the critic teaches the critic that there is something to fear. But the critic is not an enemy. It is a scared part of you.

You do not argue with a scared child. You do not try to overpower someone who is panicking or shout at a nervous helper who is doing the best they can.

You listen - notice - stay calm.

The critic starts to soften when you do not obey it and do not resist it. You let it speak without letting it control you and acknowledge it without letting it define you.

This is the first tool you learn in this book:

Let the critic speak without following its orders.

Just because a thought warns you does not mean you have to listen. You can feel fear without acting from fear, feel hesitation without letting it silence you or feeling doubt and still choose yourself.

You begin by noticing the voice exactly as it is, not as something to fight or fix.

A tiny exercise, not for change, but for awareness

Take a moment when the critic speaks today. Do not try to stop it. Just notice.

Ask yourself quietly:

What does this voice think it is protecting me from?

Not what it is saying. What it is trying to protect you from. Fear of embarrassment or fear of being wrong? Fear of not being liked or fear of being misunderstood? Fear of losing respect?

Once you see the fear behind the voice, you will understand why it speaks the way it does. It is not cruel. It is scared.

> Understanding begins to loosen its grip.

Workbook Prompts for Chapter One

Take a pen or open a blank page on your phone. Respond simply, not perfectly.

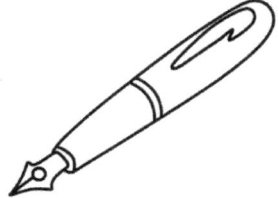

1 Write down moments today when your inner critic spoke the loudest. Small or big moments both count.

2 Write the exact words or tone it used. Was it harsh, disappointed, worried, sarcastic, quiet, tense, doubtful?

3 How did your body react? Chest, stomach, throat, face, shoulders, breathing. Just observe.

> You are not here to control the voice. You are here to notice it with honesty.

You do not need to get rid of your inner critic to build self trust. It will speak. It will warn. It will question you. You do not have to treat its anxiety like truth. You can listen without obeying. You can feel fear without living from fear.

The critic is one voice in your mind, not your identity. As you learn to understand it, you will learn to trust yourself.

In the next chapter, we explore where that voice came from and why it learned to protect you the way it does. Understanding its origins helps you take back your voice without violence or pressure. Not through courage or confidence, but through clarity and compassion toward yourself.

Self trust begins with seeing yourself clearly. You have already taken the first step.

Chapter 2
Where That Voice Came From

The inner critic sounds so personal that it is easy to believe you invented it. It speaks in the same tone as your thoughts. It uses memories you recognize. It knows exactly what scares you. So it feels like it must be you.

But it is not something you created on your own. That voice learned how to speak long before you understood what thoughts were. It copied tones you heard, rules you absorbed, expectations you tried to meet, and moments that made you feel proud or embarrassed or unseen. It took pieces of childhood, school, family beliefs, culture, and things you never questioned, and it stitched them together into one protective voice.

What you hear today is a collection of old survival lessons.

Before we talk about changing that voice or softening it, it matters to understand it. Not to blame anyone. Not to dig up hurt and hold on to it. Only to recognize how the younger version of you tried to belong, and how the critic helped you do it.

To understand the critic, we first need to understand the child who listened.

The critic formed from real moments, not just one big event

Many people assume something dramatic must have happened to shape their inner critic. They imagine a painful moment that changed everything. But for most people, the critic did not form in a single experience. It formed through repetition.

The critic learned from a pattern, not a memory.

It noticed which actions got you praise and which got you judgment. It saw which feelings were welcomed and which led to trouble. It recognized when adults looked proud and when they looked disappointed. It noticed what teachers rewarded, what friends admired, what social rules kept you accepted.

It marked these patterns as rules to follow in order to stay safe.

You did not write those rules. You just learned to live by them.

The critic stores these rules like a manual for how to exist in the world. It does not ask whether the rules are outdated. It does not check whether you still need them. It simply repeats them because that is how it learned to protect you.

If the voice feels familiar, it is because it is using a very old playbook.

How families shape the critic, even without trying

You learned early that some versions of you were easier to love than others. Not because anyone meant harm, but because every family has unspoken expectations. These expectations shape the inner critic more than any lecture.

In some families, being well behaved was valued. In others, being smart or talented earned attention. In others, being quiet kept the peace. In others, being tough or responsible was necessary. In some families, emotions were loud and messy, in others, feelings were hidden. Some homes rewarded obedience. Some rewarded independence.

As a child, you paid close attention.

You might not remember the exact moments when you learned these lessons, but your body remembers the pressure of trying to fit into the version of you that felt safest.

> Maybe someone praised you by saying you were the smart one. The quiet one. The easy one. The polite one. The strong one. The independent one. The perfect one. The calm one. The helper. The achiever. The child who never caused trouble.

Whatever role made life smoother for the family became the identity your critic tries to maintain.

Your critic is terrified of letting that role fall apart.

It is not trying to hurt you. It is trying to protect the child who learned that acceptance depended on performing a certain self.

A school moment that shaped the fear of being wrong

At some point in childhood, school began to teach that mistakes are dangerous. Not physically dangerous, but socially and intellectually risky. Being wrong meant being corrected. Being corrected meant attention. And attention did not always feel safe.

Here is a small example. Imagine a classroom. The teacher asks a question. You know the answer. At least, you think you do. You raise your hand, but as your arm lifts, you begin to doubt your clarity. Maybe you misunderstood. Maybe someone else will answer better. Maybe if you are wrong, the class will laugh or the teacher will sigh or someone will make a joke. A moment of uncertainty grows inside your body.

Your arm comes down. Another classmate answers. Their answer is the same one you had in mind. The whole moment passes in less than ten seconds, but something inside you absorbs a message:

It is safer not to be seen than to be wrong.

No one said that out loud or punished you. No one embarrassed you but yet the critic took note. It learned that waiting feels safer than risking being wrong. It learned that being correct matters more than being expressive. It learned that thinking privately is easier than speaking openly.

The critic loves safety more than honesty.

And school gave it a lot of examples to build its rules from.

Teachers, authority, and subtle fear

Teachers rarely try to make students feel small. Most of them do their best. But authority itself teaches children to measure their worth through performance. Grades measure value. Approval comes through being correct. Smart children receive attention. Mistakes are marked with red ink, as if the error is urgent.

These are not just classroom rules. They become inner rules.

The critic copies the teacher's tone. It becomes the evaluator of your choices. It looks at your decisions the same way a teacher grades your work. It tells you to double check yourself, triple check yourself, wait until you are certain, wait until you are perfect, wait until you are safe.

It wants you to earn belonging the way you once earned grades.

It is trying to help you win something that was never meant to be competed for.

Culture, identity, and what it means to be acceptable

Beyond family and school, culture shapes the critic's beliefs. Culture tells you what it means to be successful, respectable, lovable, strong, humble, or worthy. It tells you who is supposed to speak and who is supposed to stay quiet. It tells you what kind of emotions are allowed. It tells you how much confidence is acceptable before it becomes arrogance. It tells you how perfect your body should be. It tells you which dreams are ambitious and which dreams are unrealistic.

The critic listens to all of it.

In some cultures, humility is a virtue, so the critic warns you not to stand out. In others, achievement is expected, so the critic pushes you to do more and fear failure. In some communities, expressing emotions is discouraged, so the critic silences your feelings. In others, speaking boldly is demanded, so the critic shames you for being quiet.

The critic adapts itself to whatever rules help you belong.

The problem is that belonging based on performance never feels secure. You never know when you have done enough, or been enough, or worked hard enough, or earned acceptance. The critic becomes hypervigilant. It tries to constantly manage your behavior to avoid losing what it thinks is your place in the world.

The critic believes love is conditional, because that is how it learned to keep you safe.

Social media magnified the critic

The original critic came from childhood. Social media just gave it a speaker system. Now you are surrounded by proof that everyone seems to have better careers, relationships, bodies, homes, hobbies, and lives. You see people performing confidence, achievement, and beauty, and your critic tries to match those standards to keep you from falling behind.

It is the same protective instinct, just amplified.

Your critic sees a curated life and believes you need to measure up to survive. It judges your progress because it fears you will be left behind, so it compares because it thinks comparison is a strategy for staying worthy. It pushes you to impress others, not because it wants praise, but because it believes praise is protection.

The critic does not want admiration. It wants security.

It thinks the world is judging you the way school, family, and culture once did.

But the world is not doing that. The critic is.

Its purpose was protection, not harm

When you hear the critic through this lens, something begins to soften. The voice you once hated becomes more understandable. The pressure it brings makes more sense. You do not need to make war against it. You do not need to escape it. You do not need to fight it like a bully.

You can see it as a scared assistant doing a job it learned too long ago.

Think about it this way. A child without power, without independence, without control over their environment, needs protection. And the critic helped. It kept you alert when attention felt risky. It helped you behave in ways that made life smoother. It helped you avoid emotional pain you were not ready to handle. It helped you meet expectations that felt necessary at the time.

It did not know any better. But now you do.

The critic is still using the same methods with a grown person who no longer needs them. It is like a small child inside you trying to guide an adult life with a child's understanding of safety. It is not evil. It is simply outdated.

You can listen to it without letting it lead.

A softened perspective: you can update the voice

When you see the critic as a protective part, not a punishing part, you can begin to respond differently. Instead of shutting it down or obeying it, you can acknowledge it. You can recognize the fear behind it. You can respond with maturity instead of rebellion or submission.

One small practice for this chapter:

When the critic speaks, pause and say quietly in your mind:

Thank you for trying to help me. I can handle this.

Not as a performance. Not as a trick. Simply as a statement of truth. A way of telling the younger version of yourself that they do not need to control your life anymore.

You are no longer a child navigating adult expectations without tools. You can make decisions. You can face discomfort. You can survive not being perfect.

You do not need to destroy your critic to free yourself. You only need to update it.

Workbook Prompts for Chapter Two

Answer gently. This is not analysis. It is recognition.

1 Who or what shaped the tone of your inner critic?

Think of voices, silence, praise, pressure, expectations, corrections, or rules you absorbed.

2 How was perfection or achievement understood when you were growing up?

What did it mean to be good, successful, smart, respectful, worthy, or lovable?

3 What did you once wish others would say to you but never did?

Write the exact words your younger self needed to hear.

> Remember, this chapter is not about blaming the past. It is about understanding why the critic learned to protect you the way it does.

You are not breaking the voice. You are growing past it.

In the next chapter, we explore the cost of letting the voice lead your life and how fear disguised as caution slowly limits your real growth. You will begin to see how self trust offers a different path, not through perfection, but through honesty and presence.

Chapter 3
The Cost of Letting It Lead Your Life

There is a specific kind of exhaustion that does not come from working hard. It comes from doubting yourself while you are working hard. You know it well - is the tired feeling that shows up even when you have not done much, the heaviness you feel before you start something, while you are doing it, and even after you finish. The inner critic drains energy at every stage. You are not tired because your life is difficult. You are tired because your mind is busy trying to keep you safe.

This chapter looks at the cost of letting the critic lead your life. Not to make you feel guilty, and not to make you regret anything.

> Instead, this chapter is meant to help you see how much you lose when you let fear decide who you are allowed to be.

Understanding the cost is the doorway to change. If you can see clearly what the critic has been doing to your energy, your joy, your voice, and your choices, you can begin to choose differently.

The hidden drain of constant self doubt

Think about the last time you wanted to do something simple but hesitated. Maybe you wanted to send a message, start a task, speak up in a meeting, try a new activity, ask a question, or share an idea. A tiny moment where nothing serious was at stake. Before you even acted, your mind began to question you. Is this a good idea? How will it look? What if you do it wrong? Will someone judge you? Will you regret it?

This moment feels small, but it is heavy. Your brain has to sort through a storm of unnecessary warnings. That storm steals energy that should have gone into living. Self doubt takes energy before you take any action. It is like trying to drive a car while pressing the brakes the entire time. No matter how little distance you travel, it feels exhausting.

Self doubt is not just a mental habit. It becomes emotional fatigue.

The critic whispers that you need to be careful, and you freeze. It tells you to prepare more, and you overwork...to stay quiet, and you disappear. It tells you to wait for the right moment, and the right moment never comes.

Then you feel tired, and you think you are the problem, when really, you are just tired from being in constant negotiation with yourself.

Self doubt steals joy before life even begins

There is another cost, one that feels even heavier than exhaustion. Self doubt takes the joy out of living your own life. You cannot enjoy doing something if you spend the whole time judging yourself while doing it.

You cannot enjoy learning if you are afraid of looking inexperienced. You cannot enjoy rest if you feel guilty for slowing down or enjoy your accomplishments if you believe they are not enough. You also cannot enjoy creativity if your only goal is to impress someone.

The critic attaches pressure to joy and turns it into work.

The critic treats hobbies like obligations. It treats love like something you must earn. It treats progress like competition. It treats relaxation like laziness. It treats expression like a performance. It treats being yourself like a risk.

Joy does not disappear because life is boring. It disappears because the critic tries to protect you from vulnerability by controlling how free you are allowed to be.

Joy requires freedom. The critic fears freedom.

Procrastination is not laziness. It is fear.

Procrastination is one of the most misunderstood effects of the inner critic. People often think they procrastinate because they are lazy, unmotivated, or undisciplined. But procrastination almost always comes from fear. If something feels meaningful, vulnerable, uncertain, or important, self doubt shows up and stalls you.

You do not put things off because you do not care. You

put them off because you care deeply, and the critic is afraid of the outcome.

You might delay a goal because you want to do it perfectly and do not know how yet. You might delay a conversation because you fear what will happen if you speak your truth. You might delay starting a dream because the risk of failing feels too real. You might delay simple tasks because the fear of doing them imperfectly overwhelms you.

Procrastination is protection disguised as waiting.

The critic whispers that you should wait until you are certain, ready, confident, or qualified. But certainty never arrives by waiting. It arrives by beginning. The critic does not understand that. It only knows how to protect you by pausing you.

When you let fear lead your life, you spend more time preparing to live than actually living.

Over preparing is fear pretending to be responsibility

Some people do not procrastinate. Instead, they overwork and over prepare. They do more research than necessary or rehearse endlessly. They perfect every small detail, triple check what they already know or spend hours planning instead of acting. It looks responsible from the outside, but inside it is driven by fear.

> Over preparing is not driven by ambition. It is driven by the terror of being wrong.

You might think you are being diligent, wise, or careful. But the truth is that your critic is trying to protect you from potential embarrassment or failure. Preparing becomes a shield. You are not building skill. You are trying to build safety.

The critic does not know that you can handle mistakes. It believes that mistakes are threats, so it forces you to work beyond what is needed. This leads to mental exhaustion, frustration, resentment, and burnout. Not because you worked too much, but because you worked from fear.

> # Responsibility empowers you.
> # Over preparing drains you.

Burnout is not from effort. It is from emotional pressure

Burnout often comes from caring too much. You push yourself because you want to get it right. You overextend yourself because you want to meet expectations. You carry emotional pressure while doing physical or mental tasks. Effort does not burn you out. Fear burns you out.

> Burnout happens when you live like you are always being evaluated.

If your inner critic demands perfection, you will feel like nothing is enough. If it demands approval, you will feel like you need to perform for others. If it demands strength, you will feel like you cannot rest. If it demands certainty, you will feel like you are never ready.

Working from pressure is different from working from purpose. Purpose energizes. Pressure exhausts.

When the critic is in charge, success feels like relief, not pride.

Relief is temporary. Pride lasts. Relief comes from escaping a threat. Pride comes from trusting yourself.

You deserve pride, not relief.

. . .

Avoiding risks leads to a quiet life that does not feel like yours

Another cost of letting the critic lead is that your life becomes predictable, safe, and small. You avoid risks because risks bring uncertainty. You avoid new opportunities because you fear failing. You avoid vulnerability because you fear judgment. You avoid expressing yourself because you fear rejection.

Nothing bad happens. But nothing real happens either.

You do not get hurt, but you also do not get close to people...also you do not fail, but you also do not grow. You do not embarrass yourself, but you also do not feel proud. You do not make mistakes, but you also do not learn who you could be.

Avoiding risks does not protect your life. It removes life from your life.

Safety without self expression becomes numbness. You stop feeling excited. You stop feeling curious. You stop feeling connected. You stop feeling alive. The critic believes it is protecting you from pain, but it is also protecting you from joy.

A quiet life can be peaceful, but it can also feel lonely when it is quiet for the wrong reasons.

You are not meant to avoid your own life.

Doubt blocks creativity and the freedom to express yourself

Creativity is not reserved for artists. Creativity is part of being human. It shows up when you solve a problem, share an idea, make something new, express a feeling, change your life, try something for fun, or admit a truth you have been hiding.

The critic interferes with creativity in many ways. It tells you your ideas are not original enough. It tells you your thoughts are not interesting. It tells you your work is not good enough. It tells you other people will do it better. It tells you to edit yourself before you even begin.

Creativity cannot breathe when fear is in charge.

Ideas cannot grow if you judge them before they exist. Opinions cannot form if you are scared to express them. Passions cannot develop if you expect perfection on the first try. You cannot discover what you are capable of if you believe you must impress someone every time you create.

Creativity needs space to fail, play, and explore. The critic does not allow that. It thinks freedom is irresponsible. But freedom is how humans learn, connect, and develop their voice.

You cannot build confidence in a skill without letting yourself be imperfect at it. Hiding your ideas does not protect you from failure. It protects you from becoming yourself.

You lose more from not trying than from being wrong

This is the truth the critic cannot see. You can recover from embarrassment and you can learn from failure. You can heal from rejection, correct a mistake, or rebuild your confidence. You can grow after being wrong, but you cannot get back the moments you never lived.

You cannot learn from silence, cannot love without vulnerability. You cannot become skilled without practice or t build relationships without honesty. You cannot discover your path without risking missteps and cannot know your potential if you refuse to begin.

When fear leads, life becomes something you observe rather than something you participate in.

Mistakes hurt, but regret lasts longer. Vulnerability is uncomfortable, but hiding yourself hurts more. Failure is temporary, but playing small can last a lifetime. Taking risks brings uncertainty, but living without risk brings emptiness.

You deserve a life that comes from choosing yourself, not protecting yourself.

Trusting yourself is a skill, not a personality trait

Here is the hopeful shift. Trust is not something you either have or do not have. It is something you build through experience. Trust grows when you make choices and live through them. It grows when you express yourself and survive the discomfort, or when you take small risks and see that nothing terrible happens. Trust grows when you follow your own voice, not someone else's expectations.

You do not need to feel confident to act. Confidence is the result of acting. You do not need to know the outcome to choose. Choices create outcomes. You do not need to be fearless. You only need to stop letting fear decide everything.

Self trust is built through action, not perfection.

Every time you speak even when you are unsure, you grow trust. When you try something new and allow yourself to be imperfect, you grow trust, or when you take a step without knowing how it will end, you grow trust. Every time you show your real self instead of your safe self, you grow trust.

Trust is not a feeling you wait for. Trust is a relationship you build with yourself.

A gentle beginning

You do not need to flip a switch. You do not need to transform your life in one big moment. You do not need to become bold, loud, or fearless. You simply need to stop letting fear lead your decisions. You can let doubt exist without letting it control you.

The next time you catch yourself preparing too much, waiting too long, or shrinking when you want to speak, you can pause and ask:

What if I trust myself for one moment?

Not for a lifetime. Not for a year. Not even for a day. Just for one moment.

Trust begins with small choices. Small honesty. Small risks. Small truths. Small steps. Every small moment of trust becomes a brick in the foundation of a more confident life. Not confident because you never feel fear anymore. Confident because you no longer treat fear as authority.

Fear can come with you. It just cannot lead.

Workbook Prompts for Chapter Three

Answer slowly and honestly.

1 What has self doubt stopped you from doing?

Think of any moment you held back, avoided, or waited.

2 Write about one missed moment that still nags you.

Do not judge yourself. Just describe how it felt to let that moment pass.

3 Imagine how that moment would have gone if you trusted yourself.

Not perfectly. Not impressively. Just honestly. How would it feel to show up as you?

There is no correct answer. There is only truth. And truth builds trust.

> Doubt protected you, but it also restricted you.

You do not need to fight it. You only need to stop letting it lead. A life run by fear is not a safe life. It is a small one. You deserve more than safety. You deserve to experience your life.

In the next chapter, we explore the difference between confidence and self trust. You will learn why you do not need to feel strong to act with intention, and why the smallest choices can transform your identity. The journey ahead is not about becoming fearless. It is about becoming free.

Chapter 4
Self Trust Is Not Confidence

Most of us are taught to chase confidence. We are told that confidence will make life easier. We hear that confident people speak up, take risks, move boldly, and never worry about how they are seen. We imagine confidence as a kind of inner power. Something bright. Something noticeable. Something loud enough to silence every doubt.

Yet when we look closely, confidence is not what helps a person build a steady life. Confidence can be loud, but loudness is not the same as strength. It can impress others for a moment, but impressing others is not the same as belonging to yourself. Confidence can appear powerful, but appearance is not the same as stability or it may look like certainty, but certainty is not always available in real life.

What we need more than confidence is self trust.

Confidence	Self Trust
Confidence asks us to feel sure of ourselves.	Trust asks us to act from ourselves.
Confidence wants proof first.	Trust is willing to begin without it.
Confidence focuses on how we look to others.	Trust focuses on how we are with ourselves.
Confidence attracts attention.	Trust does not need attention to exist.
Confidence might come and go.	Trust can stay steady.
Confidence is often loud or showy.	Self trust is quiet, steady, and grounded.
Confidence is about performance.	Trust is about alignment with who we are.
Confidence believes success means being right.	Trust believes we can handle what comes, even without knowing the outcome.

Some people try to find confidence before they live their lives. They wait to feel strong before they take a step. They hope an inner certainty will magically arrive, as if confidence is permission. But waiting for confidence has prevented many experiences. It has delayed growth, held back expression, silenced honesty, and turned life into preparation instead of participation.

Self trust asks something different. It does not require loudness. It does not ask for certainty. It only asks that we stay with ourselves through the unknown.

Confidence is loud, trust is quiet

> Many people mistaken confidence for power because confidence is easier to see.

It often comes with a raised voice, fast opinions, or showmanship. It can look impressive. Someone who seems confident may take up space, speak without hesitation, share bold ideas, or act decisively.

This can be useful at times, but it does not always reflect inner steadiness.

> Quietness is often misunderstood as insecurity.

A quiet person may think deeply, ask questions, take time to respond, or move slowly before acting. Their strength is internal, not external. They do not need to perform certainty. They do not need to look daring. They are not rushing to prove themselves. Their steadiness comes from within.

> Confidence tries to convince the world. Trust does not need convincing.

A confident voice might make others notice. A trusting heart makes decisions without asking to be noticed. A confident person might say, "I can do this because I believe in myself." A trusting person might say, "I will do this because it matters to me." One is guided by a feeling of superiority or boldness. The other is guided by alignment.

> Trust does not show off.
> It does not need to.

You do not need confidence to act with trust

We learn to believe that action should come after certainty. But life does not wait for certainty. Most meaningful actions are done while feeling unsure. A first step is rarely taken from confidence. It is taken from willingness.

When people start something new, they often do not know what they are doing. A person taking care of a newborn does not begin with confidence. They begin with love and a willingness to learn. A person starting a creative practice does not begin with mastery. They begin with curiosity. A person who tries a new skill does not begin knowing they will succeed. They begin because something inside them asks to try.

Trust acts while uncertainty is present. Confidence waits for uncertainty to disappear.

If someone waits to feel confident before taking action, they may wait forever. Confidence often arrives after experience, not before it. It appears after we begin, not as a prerequisite.

Self trust allows us to begin without feeling ready. It allows quiet movement. It respects our pace. It accepts mistakes as part of the process. It builds resilience, not performance.

Trust says, "I do not know the outcome, but I will stay with myself whatever the outcome is."

Confidence tries to guarantee success. Trust guarantees presence.

Presence matters more.

Confidence wants to prove your worth. Trust honors it

Confidence can sometimes feel like an attempt to prove something. It can turn action into performance. It can turn conversations into competition. It can make effort a display. Many people confuse worth with visible achievement. They believe they must prove themselves through things others can see.

Trust does not ask us to perform value. Trust recognizes that value already exists.

A trusting person does not try to show they are intelligent, they simply share their thoughts. They do not try to show they are capable, they simply do what they need to do. Their life is not a presentation. It is an expression of who they are and what matters to them.

Trust does not chase approval. It protects alignment.

Confidence feels pressured by the presence of others. Trust feels grounded regardless of the audience. Confidence can disappear when attention fades. Trust remains when no one is watching.

Worth is not earned through external performance. Worth is respected through internal alignment. When a person trusts themselves, they honor their worth through the choices they make, not the reactions they receive.

Self trust is the quiet decision to stand with yourself, even when no one else is watching.

A story about someone who trusts themselves quietly

There was a man who worked in a small local store. He was not loud, and he was not seeking attention. He moved slowly, but not out of hesitation. He listened carefully when people spoke to him. He asked questions when he was unsure. He did not pretend to know things he did not know. When customers rushed him, he stayed calm. When someone became impatient, he did not react with defensiveness. He continued to do his work with patience.

Outside the store, he spent time gardening. Not professionally. Not to get recognition. He liked growing things. He planted seeds and learned through trial and error. Some plants thrived, some did not. He did not talk about it much. He did not show pictures of his progress. He simply cared for the plants because he enjoyed the process. There was no need to impress anyone.

People often mistook his calm for quietness or shyness. But his steadiness came from a simple truth. He did not need to rush to prove himself. He did not need to pretend to know more than he did. He did not need to make his interests impressive. He had no pressure to perform. His choices were not reactions to others. They were expressions of what mattered to him.

Nothing about him demanded attention, yet most people trusted him without thinking about why. His reliability came from being aligned with himself. He did not move fast, but he moved with clarity. He did not try to seem strong, but others experienced him as strong. He did not seek admiration, yet his presence inspired quiet respect.

This is what trust looks like. It does not compete. It does not advertise itself. It does not require certainty. It simply moves from a place of self alignment.

Trust turns ordinary actions into grounded living.

The goal is not to be bold, but to be grounded

Many try to become bolder, louder, more fearless, more impressive. They believe growth is measured in volume. Yet boldness without grounding can still be fragile. People can shout their opinions and still feel insecure. They can take dramatic risks and still feel lost. They can move quickly and still have no idea who they are.

Groundedness is different. A grounded person knows what matters to them. They know what they value. They know what they refuse. They know what they want to support and what they cannot participate in. They do not need to be dramatic with their boundaries. They do not need to make their choices a statement. They simply live in alignment with their own values.

The goal of this book is not to help anyone become fearless or flashy. It is not to encourage grand gestures or perfect confidence. The goal is to help a person become stable enough inside that they can live their life on their own terms. Not loudly. Not to impress. Simply to be honest with themselves.

Real growth is not about becoming more noticeable. It is about becoming more rooted.

A grounded person can act without being certain. They can speak without trying to dominate. They can work without trying to prove worth. They can express themselves without fear of performing. They can love without pretending. They can create without demands. They can rest without guilt.

Groundedness is self trust turned into daily life.

A new definition of strength

Strength is often pictured as something firm, loud, or dramatic. But strength can also be quiet. Strength does not need to overpower anyone. Strength does not prove itself. Strength does not need to win. Strength simply remains aligned.

Strength is sticking to your values even if others disagree. To choose honesty when silence would be easier. Strength is letting go of performance and choosing authenticity, to act without guarantees or allowing yourself to be imperfect while still showing up. Strength is living from your own truth rather than chasing validation. Its not a posture. It is a relationship with your own choices.

Trust is not about feeling strong. It is about staying with yourself when things are hard, confusing, emotional, or uncertain. A person who trusts themselves does not collapse inside when doubt appears. They hear the doubt, they feel the uncertainty, and they continue anyway. They stay present with themselves.

Strength is staying present with yourself.

. . .

Workbook Prompts for Chapter Four

Answer these gently, without trying to be clever or profound.

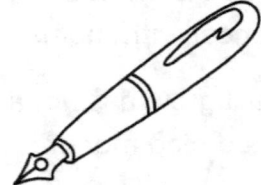

1 Describe someone in your life who is quietly sure of themselves. What makes their presence feel steady without being loud or attention seeking?

2 What does self trust feel like in your body? Where does it rest? How does it feel physically when you know something is true for you?

3 Write a short promise to yourself that is easy to keep. Not a goal. Not a performance. A promise. Something small that honors who you are.

Examples of the spirit of a promise might be: I will pause before abandoning myself. I will listen to what I need. I will not rush to prove anything.

Your promise does not need to impress anyone. It only needs to be true.

Confidence might look appealing, but trust is what carries us through life. Confidence wants attention. Trust wants alignment. Confidence tries to prove. Trust wants to honor. Confidence can come and go. Trust can grow steadily through experience.

The strength you are searching for is not somewhere outside you, waiting in a future version of yourself. It is something you build by choosing yourself in small, quiet, grounded ways.

In the next chapter, we explore how to turn the inner critic into a guide instead of a judge. This is where compassion for the scared part of ourselves becomes a tool for clarity. Trust deepens not by silencing the critic, but by listening differently.

Chapter 5
Turning the Critic into a Guide

There is a strange thing many people learn to do with their inner critic. They either obey it completely or try to get rid of it. Some spend years trying to silence the voice. Others spend years obeying its warnings as if the critic knows something they do not. Both strategies make sense.

Trying to silence the critic often makes it louder. Trying to obey it makes life smaller. Neither one feels good. Silence is exhausting. Obedience is limiting. There has to be another way. There is. It begins with curiosity.

> Curiosity is the secret most people never try because curiosity sounds surprisingly boring.

It is not flashy enough to feel like a solution. It does not sound powerful, like fighting the critic. It does not sound safe, like obeying the critic. Curiosity sounds slow. Plain. Calm. But that is why it works.

Curiosity changes the tone of the entire inner world. It invites the critic to speak honestly without letting it lead. It treats the critic as something worth understanding, not something to destroy or worship. This is how the critic begins to shift from judge to guide.

Why fighting or obeying does not work

When we treat the critic as a problem that must be defeated, our mind becomes a battlefield. The critic says, "You might embarrass yourself." We shout back, "Stop thinking that." It says, "You are not ready." We respond, "Be confident." The critic panics, so we panic about panicking. This creates two anxious voices instead of one.

Fighting the critic gives it power. It teaches the critic that its warnings are dangerous enough to be confronted. That makes the voice louder. It now thinks there must be something serious to worry about if we are reacting so strongly. The inner critic believes danger is real because we act like it is real.

Obeying the critic has its own cost. When the critic warns us, we withdraw. We wait. We shrink. We over prepare. We silence ourselves. The critic learns that its warnings shape our behavior. That makes the critic feel responsible for our protection. It tries harder to protect us. It becomes stricter, louder, more reactive.

In both cases, the critic learns the same message: what it says is important.

Neither fighting nor obeying teaches the critic anything new. Both encourage fear. Both assume the critic knows something we do not. Both accept that doubt is a sign of danger.

What would happen if instead of treating the critic as a threat or authority, we treated it like a confused coworker who means well but does not know how to do your job? You would not fight that person. You would not hand them your responsibilities. You would probably start asking questions.

. . .

A new approach: question the voice

Questioning the critic is not the same as arguing with it. Arguing tries to shut the voice down. Questioning tries to understand it. When we question, we are not trying to win. We are trying to see beneath the words. Most people assume the critic is cruel. But cruelty is rarely its real intention. The critic speaks harshly because it is afraid.

> Harshness is fear wearing armor.

When the critic tells someone not to speak, it is trying to protect them from humiliation. When it tells someone their work is not good enough, it is trying to protect them from judgment. When it tells someone to wait until they are ready, it is trying to protect them from failure.

Questioning reveals the intention behind the critic's tone. Instead of asking "Why does this voice attack me?" we can ask "What is this voice afraid of?" The intention matters more than the tone.

Here are three simple questions to ask the critic. Not in a dramatic way. Not like a ritual. Just with honest curiosity.

1 What is this voice afraid will happen?

2 Who taught it to protect me this way?

3 Is this fear still true for my life now?

These questions create space. They take the pressure off. They give you time to listen without obeying. You are not trying to calm the critic. You are simply trying to understand what it is trying to do.

When the critic feels understood, it does something interesting. It begins to speak less like a judge and more like someone offering advice, even if the advice is clumsy. That shift matters more than silencing the voice ever could.

· · ·

Responding with curiosity instead of pressure

Curiosity does not need force. It does not need hype. It does not need a motivational speech. Curiosity simply listens and asks for clarity. This gives us room to choose our actions instead of reacting automatically.

Imagine the critic says, "Do not share your idea. People will think it is stupid." Many people respond in one of two ways. They either obey silently, shrinking inside, or they yell back in their mind, "Stop being negative. I am smart. I should think positive." Both responses carry stress. Both treat the critic as a threat or a tyrant. But what if instead we simply asked the voice a question?

"What are you trying to protect me from?"

The critic might answer internally, "Embarrassment." Suddenly, the critic looks less like a bully and more like a nervous guardian that has no idea how to calm down. It stops sounding like the enemy and starts sounding like a scared assistant. And scared assistants do not need to be fired. They need direction.

Curiosity makes the critic less intimidating. It also makes your inner world less dramatic. No shouting. No shutting down. Just understanding. And from understanding comes choice.

We do not have to obey fear just because we understand it. Understanding the fear allows us to choose responsibly instead of automatically. Understanding is not permission for fear to lead. Understanding is the beginning of leadership.

Transforming harsh criticism into useful information

Once we understand the intention behind the critic's message, we can transform it. The message does not need to be thrown away. It needs to be translated. Criticism always contains information. It just delivers it poorly.

Think of the critic as someone who has important data but has no idea how to communicate appropriately. The data itself is not the problem. The delivery is what causes pain.

Let us look at a few examples.

Harsh Critic Message	Real Intention	Useful Translation
"You will fail."	Avoid disappointment	Prepare thoughtfully, then try.
"People will judge you."	Avoid rejection	Share with people who matter, not everyone.
"This is not good enough."	Avoid shame	Improve one part, then move forward.
"You do not know what you are doing."	Avoid embarrassment	Ask for help or learn as you go.
"Wait until you are ready."	Avoid risk	Take one step now, learn the rest by doing.

When we translate the critic, we do not lose caution. Caution becomes strategy instead of fear. Fear becomes information instead of control. Instead of pushing fear away or letting it dominate, we treat it as a messenger with a terrible communication style.

The critic says, "Do not do this." The message underneath is often, "I am afraid you will get hurt." Once we see the fear, we can respond with clarity instead of panic. We can say to ourselves, "Thank you for your concern. I will take care of us."

> That is leadership. Not silence. Not surrender.
> Leadership.

The critic is not you

This is the moment where many people begin to feel relief. When they realize that the critic is not their identity, something softens. The critic is not your personality, its not your weakness, not your true voice. The critic is a protective part that has learned old rules.

This voice was built from early survival strategies. It learned to protect you before you had the skills to protect yourself. It speaks with outdated fear. It believes life is still dangerous in the same ways it was when you were young. It does not understand that you are an adult now.

The critic is simply a scared part of your history that is trying to guide the present using outdated instructions. It is like a child who learned to warn you long before you gained emotional and practical tools. The child inside still believes it is responsible for your safety, without realizing you have changed.

You do not need to destroy this part. You can lead it gently. You can give it updated information. You can show it that you can handle mistakes. That you can handle being imperfect. That you can handle sadness, disappointment, differences, success, failure, love, risk, and vulnerability.

>You can handle life. The critic does not know that yet.

Let your wiser self lead

There is another voice inside, although it might not speak as loudly. It does not shout, does not make threats and does not demand perfection. It does not panic, and is not dramatic. It is calm. Sometimes quiet, and other times gentle. Sometimes just a feeling in the body that says, "This is right for me."

This voice is the wiser version of you. It is not a motivational coach, and does not try to hype you up. It does not care about being convincing - It cares about alignment. It wants you to act from your values, not your fears.

Trust Yourself Anyway

The wiser voice is steady, not loud. It is honest. It does not pretend to know everything, but it trusts that you will figure things out along the way. It does not expect you to be perfect. It accepts mistakes as part of the journey. It does not ask you to impress anyone. It asks you to stay present with yourself.

When the critic speaks, instead of reacting, we can invite the wiser voice to respond. Not to argue. Not to shut the critic down. Just to offer perspective.

For example:

Critic: "Do not do this, you might fail."

Wiser Self: "If I fail, I can learn."

Critic: "People might judge you."

Wiser Self: "People have their own lives. I will live mine."

Critic: "This is not perfect yet."

Wiser Self: "It does not need to be perfect to matter."

These responses are not hype. They are grounded. They express trust without pretending to be fearless. They speak with maturity. The critic is afraid of outcomes. The wiser self trusts the process.

Trust is not a belief in success. Trust is a belief in your ability to navigate whatever happens next.

Workbook Prompts for Chapter Five

Take time with these. Let your answers be simple and honest.

1 Write a critical thought, then rewrite it as a protective but clumsy message.

Example structure: Harsh version: "You are not ready." Protective version: "I want you to feel safe."

2 What is the critic trying to prevent? Shame, judgment, rejection, failure, embarrassment, loss, attention, vulnerability. Write what you sense underneath the message.

3 What would a wiser, calmer version of you say instead? Not loud. Not exaggerated. Just a grounded response that supports your next step.

The critic is not your enemy. It is a scared voice that has been trying too hard to protect you. When we treat it with curiosity, we stop reacting from fear and start acting from clarity. When we translate its warnings, we stop shrinking and start choosing. When we let our wiser self lead, we stop performing and start aligning.

You do not need to fight the critic or obey it. You can learn from it. You can guide it. You can show it that life is not as delicate as it once believed.

Trust grows when fear loses its authority, not its voice.

In the next chapter, we explore how small acts of courage build self trust, not through confidence, but through quiet follow through. The smallest decisions can change the way you see yourself.

Chapter 6
Small Acts of Courage Build Self Trust

Most people imagine courage as something dramatic. Climbing mountains. Starting big companies. Telling off a crowd. Quitting everything to follow a dream. Courage gets advertised as loud, bold, even glamorous. Yet for many of us, the bravest moments are surprisingly small. They are quiet choices that barely make a sound. They are decisions that matter to us, even when no one else sees them.

Like choosing to rest even when your mind says you should keep going, or drinking water when you have been ignoring your body all day. Something like saying no when something drains you or deciding you will not solve someone else's problem for the seventh time this week.

These moments may not look heroic. They do not go on social media. No one applauds. No one gives you a trophy. But these tiny decisions change who you become.

> Self trust grows through these small acts of courage.
> Not through performance.

Not through big leaps. Not through dramatic transformation. Quiet follow through builds inner strength.

There is something powerful about doing a small thing you promised yourself you would do. It might feel insignificant in the moment. But that small decision is evidence. It is proof that you can count on yourself. Not perfectly. Not impressively. Simply reliably.

Trust is built through small choices

When people feel stuck in their lives, they often wait for something big to happen. A big moment of bravery, a big change or a big realization. They keep waiting for the perfect time to start taking care of themselves, for a burst of confidence before they try something new. They keep waiting for clarity before saying what they really feel. Waiting becomes a habit. Hope turns into delay.

Life rarely changes through big moments. Life changes because of small follow through.

Think of all the things people do every day that require zero confidence, yet create meaningful change:

- taking five minutes to breathe before reacting
- drinking a glass of water in the morning
- stretching even when stiff or tired
- resting without guilt when the body feels worn out
- choosing sleep instead of scrolling
- eating a meal before you get irritable instead of after
- saying no to something you never wanted in the first place

None of these are heroic. Yet each one says, in a quiet way, "I matter enough to care for myself." That is the essence of self trust. Not performing strength. Honoring your needs.

Self trust grows when we keep small promises to ourselves. If the promises are huge, overwhelming, or unrealistic, we do not keep them. Then we lose trust. If the promises are tiny and human, we keep them. Then trust grows.

> ## Small is not a downgrade.
> ## Small is sustainable.

Courage is not big or loud

The loud version of courage is exciting to imagine. The quiet version is much more common. Quiet courage is less about proving something and more about protecting something. It protects your time, your needs, your body, your mind, your energy, and your well being.

Quiet courage sounds like: "I need to rest now" or "I will not rush myself." These statements do not require shouting. They do not require a motivational speech. They just require honesty. Honesty itself is courageous, especially when we are used to ignoring our needs, pushing ourselves too hard, or trying to meet expectations we never agreed to.

Here are a few small acts of courage that look ordinary to others but are meaningful inside:

- closing yourlaptop at a reasonable hour
- leaving dishes for later because your body needs a break
- saying no to a favor that drains you

These actions might seem tiny, but something happens when you choose them. You feel more like a person instead of a machine. You remember that you are not here to perform productivity. You are here to live.

. . .

Identity is shaped by small decisions

Most people think identity is shaped by personality, beliefs, goals, or experiences. While those things matter, identity is built in a much simpler way. You become who you are through what you repeatedly do.

If someone consistently interrupts their own needs, they become someone who does not matter to themselves. Not because they lack value, but because they keep abandoning their needs. If someone consistently chooses small moments of care, they become someone who values themselves. Not because they are perfect, but because they follow through.

Identity does not grow from intention. Identity grows from repetition.

Imagine a person who keeps saying yes when they mean no. Over time, they become someone who feels obligated rather than free. They become overwhelmed, resentful, and disconnected from their own needs. They might look helpful on the outside, but inside they feel invisible to themselves.

Now imagine a person who begins practicing tiny boundaries. Nothing confrontational. Nothing dramatic. Just small decisions like: choosing not to respond to every request immediately, not scheduling themselves beyond their energy or leaving a group conversation when they feel drained.

These actions slowly change how they see themselves.

They begin to feel that their needs matter. They begin to feel that they are allowed to exist without constant giving. They begin to feel that time and energy are things they can choose, not things that are taken from them. This is how identity reshapes quietly.

Success is not the point. Follow through is.

> People often confuse success with growth. Success is an outcome. Growth is a process.

Self trust has very little to do with success and everything to do with follow through. You can fail and still build trust. You can succeed and still lose trust.

If you rest when you need rest, even if your to do list is full, you build self trust. If you try a new habit imperfectly but continue anyway, you also build self trust. Follow through is what matters, not applause. Follow through is what matters, not perfection. Follow through is what matters, not speed. Follow through is the moment where you choose yourself instead of abandoning yourself.

When someone follows through on small choices that matter to them, they do not need confidence. They do not need to feel strong. They simply need to be consistent enough to show themselves that they are a person who keeps their word.

> Confidence waits for certainty. Self trust grows through action.

Small personal care is a form of courage

Caring for yourself is not always easy. Some people do not rest because they are scared of being useless. Some do not eat when hungry because they are used to putting work first. Some do not take breaks because they are afraid of being judged as lazy. Some do not slow down because they believe their value depends on constant achievement.

Personal care is not weakness. Personal care is self respect.

Small acts of care are statements. They say:

- my needs matter even when they are simple
- I will not ignore my body to meet expectations
- I choose to treat myself as someone worth caring for

This does not mean long spa days or elaborate rituals. It means listening. Listening to your body, your energy, your limits. Listening before the breaking point, when you need sleep instead of caffeine or when you need hydration instead of distraction. Listening when you need a pause instead of a push.

> Caring for yourself is a series of micro agreements that say, "I will not abandon me today."

Small boundaries are emotional self respect

Boundaries are not always big confrontations. Sometimes a boundary is quiet. It is the decision not to help when you are exhausted. It is turning your phone face down so you are not always available. It is ignoring a message until you have the energy to respond. It is not explaining why you cannot do something. It is not taking on someone else's emotional load.

> Boundaries protect energy, not relationships. Healthy relationships can handle boundaries.

Healthy people do not demand access to all your time and attention. Boundaries do not push people away. They simply keep you included in your own life.

Small boundaries also prove something important. They show that you do not need to justify your limits. You do not need to ask permission to care for yourself. You do not need to earn rest by giving too much first. You are allowed to choose what you have capacity for.

This is quiet courage. Not dramatic. Not angry. Just honest.

Follow through even when it is small

Following through on small promises is how your mind learns that you are dependable. It is how the nervous system relaxes. When you continuously abandon yourself, anxiety grows because you do not know if you will protect your well being when life gets overwhelming. When you consistently honor yourself in small moments, anxiety decreases because your inner world begins to trust your decisions.

Following through does not mean perfect habits. It means small consistency. Small consistency creates internal stability. Internal stability creates resilience. Once self trust begins to take root, confidence becomes optional. You do not need to feel confident because you are dependable to yourself.

This dependability changes everything.

You become someone who does not need urgency to act. Someone who does not need validation to follow through. Someone who does not need perfection to participate. Someone who does not abandon themselves when things get hard.

When you honor small promises, you become someone you can rely on.

Workbook Prompts for Chapter Six

Choose simplicity. Let the goal be follow through, not performance.

1 Choose a small daily promise for the next seven days. Make it realistic, clear, and easy to honor.

Examples:

- drink one glass of water in the morning
- stretch for three minutes
- leave one message unanswered until you have capacity

2 List five things worth doing poorly. These are things that matter even if they are messy, simple, or imperfect.

Examples might include:

- speaking honestly
- resting when tired
- cooking something basic

3 Track how you feel when you follow through, even a little. Write a few words or a sentence each day describing what it felt like to choose yourself.

Examples:

- "I felt calmer after saying no"
- "It was awkward but freeing"
- "I actually felt proud of that tiny step"

Self trust does not begin with big gestures. It begins with small agreements. It begins with caring for yourself in ordinary ways. It begins with boundaries that quietly protect your energy. It begins with following through when no one is watching. These moments seem insignificant, but they are shaping something meaningful. They are shaping a life that includes you.

A life built on small promises is stronger than a life full of grand intentions.

A life that honors needs is richer than a life built on performance.

A life with gentle boundaries is a life where you finally belong to yourself.

Little acts of courage change how you see yourself. One tiny promise at a time, you become someone you can trust.

Chapter 7
Let Yourself Be Seen Imperfectly

Perfection sounds safe in theory. It promises protection. If everything looks polished, if every word is measured, if every idea is flawless, nothing bad can happen. No embarrassment, no rejection, no criticism. Perfection tries to protect you from discomfort. The problem is that perfection does this by hiding you. A person can be cleanly edited on the outside and completely unseen on the inside.

Perfectionism is less about high standards and more about fear wearing a tidy outfit. It is the fear of being known. The fear of being judged. The fear of showing up without a script. Perfection wants to control how others see you. Vulnerability asks you to be who you are, not who you think they want.

The strange irony is that perfection prevents the very connection it tries to protect.

> You cannot be loved for who you are if you never show who you are.

A polished version of you may be accepted, but the real you will still feel alone.

Being seen imperfectly is not about being sloppy. It is about being honest. It is about letting the truth be visible, even if the truth is awkward, incomplete, emotional, unsure, or messy.

Perfectionism hides you from connection

Perfectionism can make life feel like a performance. You rehearse conversations in your mind, or rewrite messages over and over. You try to find the perfect response so that no one misunderstands you, or try to look like you know what you are doing even when you are confused.

> You try to do things perfectly so no one sees how human you are.

Here is a small example many people know too well. Someone asks how you feel. You do not know how to answer honestly, so you say something simple like, "I am fine" or "I am busy, but it is all good." Meanwhile a real answer sits in your chest, asking for air. Something like, "I am tired" or "I am sad today" or "I need a little space." The real answer is sensitive. The real answer makes you visible. So perfection covers it with something tidy.

Another example. You want to share a creative idea. A drawing, a project, a thought, a plan. Instead of sharing, you keep editing and editing. The idea never sees the light because you are protecting it from imperfect exposure. The result looks safe. No one critiques you. No one judges you. But you also never get the connection, support, or growth that comes from showing your creativity in progress.

> Perfectionism is a form of loneliness. It allows people to see your results, but not your heart.

Being seen imperfectly builds self trust

Trust is built when you allow yourself to exist, not perform. When you speak honestly, even if your voice wobbles a little or when you share something unfinished instead of waiting until you have mastered it. When you say no, even if you do not sound like a boundary expert.

Self trust grows when you show up as a real human - when you ask for help without trying to look strong, you trust that you are allowed to need things.

You do not need to be graceful. You only need to be honest.

Honesty is a form of self respect. It says, "I am willing to stand with myself, as I am, not as a performance." When you show yourself, you are no longer abandoning yourself to protect an image. You are no longer hiding behind perfection as if it is safer to disappear than to risk being seen.

Stories of imperfect expression

To make this more real, let us look at a few imperfect, beautifully human moments.

The awkward communicator.

A person tries to express a need to a friend. They have rehearsed their sentence in their head, but when the words come out, they sound slightly clumsy. Something like, "I really love hanging out, but I think I need quiet time tonight." Their delivery is unsure. Their face gets warm. But the friend responds kindly. Not because the sentence was perfect, but because the person was honest.

The unfinished creator.

Someone shares a half written poem with a friend. The lines do not all make sense. The rhythm is uneven. They feel nervous. But the friend reads it and says, "This part right here is beautiful." They feel seen, not because they created something flawless, but because they dared to share something real in progress.

The boundary beginner.

A person says no to a request from a coworker. The no is too soft. The explanation is too long. They feel like they sounded apologetic instead of firm. But they said no anyway. Later they feel a little proud, even if it was awkward. That awkwardness is the sound of a boundary being born.

These moments are not perfect. That is the point. They are real. Imperfect expression gives other people the chance to meet who you actually are. Imperfect expression gives you the chance to meet yourself.

Imperfection is evidence of action

A perfect idea remains unshared. A perfect message is never sent. A perfect painting sits in someone's head for years because they will not put paint to paper until they know exactly how to do it. A perfect boundary never gets spoken. A perfect project remains a dream.

> The world is full of perfect ideas that never lived
> because fear wanted them flawless.

If something is imperfect, it means you began. It means you participated. It means you stepped into the world instead of only thinking about it inside your mind. Imperfection is evidence of movement.

This applies to creativity, relationships, communication, rest, learning, love, boundaries, and honesty.

- A messy sketch proves you tried to create.
- A clumsy sentence proves you attempted honesty.

- A shaky voice proves you expressed yourself.

It is tempting to see imperfection as a failure. But imperfection is a sign that you are living. Perfection is a sign that you are hiding.

Being real in small ways

You do not need to become boldly vulnerable. You do not need to spill your entire heart to everyone or to post your struggles online or expose your deepest secrets. Letting yourself be seen imperfectly can begin quietly and safely. It can happen in small gestures of honesty.

Here are a few simple ways someone might let themselves be seen:

- Admitting they are tired without adding an apology
- Saying, "I do not understand" in a group conversation
- Sharing an unfinished idea with a trusted person

These are not dramatic. There is no spotlight. Yet each one shows you something important. It shows that you are willing to live your life honestly, not perform it.

A simple sentence to choose honesty over perfection

When the critic tries to make you perfect, it is not trying to ruin your life. It is trying to prevent something uncomfortable. It wants to protect you from awkwardness, embarrassment, and disapproval. Instead of obeying it or arguing with it, you can speak a grounding sentence to yourself.

The sentence does not need to be impressive. It just needs to help you stay with yourself. Here are a few options:

- "It is okay to show up as I am."

- "This is how I begin."
- "I choose honesty, not performance."

Choose one sentence to repeat when you feel the urge to hide behind perfection. Choose one that feels like comfort, not pressure. One that supports your humanity, not your performance.

Workbook Prompts for Chapter Seven

These are small exercises meant to practice being seen in safe, imperfect ways.

1 Share something imperfect with someone safe this week. It could be an idea, a feeling, a creative draft, a boundary, or a half finished effort.

2 Write about a moment when someone appreciated your honesty. Reflect on what it felt like to be understood, not for being impressive, but for being real.

3 Create a simple sentence you can use when you choose honesty over perfection. This sentence is not a performance. It is a quiet promise to yourself.

You do not need to perfect yourself to belong. You need to allow yourself to be visible in ways that are true. You do not need to impress the people who care about you. You just need to let them see who you are. Imperfection does not block connection. It is the doorway to it.

Connection happens through honesty, not through performance. Self trust grows when you stop hiding behind perfection and begin to live as a real, imperfect, breathing human being.

You are not here to create a flawless version of yourself. You are here to show up as someone alive.

Chapter 8
A Life You Can Trust Yourself In

There is a kind of life that does not require you to impress anyone to feel at peace. A life where your decisions are not shaped by fear, by perfection, or by the need to be admired. A life where your voice matters to you, even if it is quiet. A life where you are not performing who you think you should be, but living from who you are.

> This kind of life is not built through dramatic change or fearless leaps. It grows slowly, almost shyly, through honest choices.

It grows when you begin to live as someone who deserves their own care. It grows when you stop abandoning yourself every time fear shows up. It grows when you listen for your real voice and treat it like something worth respecting.

A life you can trust yourself in does not begin when you become perfect. It begins when you stop leaving yourself behind.

There is a kind of life that does not require you to impress anyone to feel at peace. A life where your decisions are not shaped by fear, by perfection, or by the need to be admired. A life where your voice matters to you, even if it is quiet. A life where you are not performing who you think you should be, but living from who you are.

This kind of life is not built through dramatic change or fearless leaps. It grows slowly, almost shyly, through honest choices. It grows when you begin to live as someone who deserves their own care. It grows when you stop abandoning yourself every time fear shows up. It grows when you listen for your real voice and treat it like something worth respecting.

A life you can trust yourself in does not begin when you become perfect. It begins when you stop leaving yourself behind.

A life that feels like home

Many people dream about a future version of themselves. A happier self. A calmer self or a more successful self. They imagine that one day, after enough achievement or healing or discipline, they will finally feel like they belong in their lives. They picture a day when their inner voice becomes peaceful, their relationships become easy, and their identity is certain.

But life does not wait for final versions. You do not need to become a new person to live a trustworthy life. You simply need to stop building your life for other people's approval and begin building it from your own truth.

> A trustworthy life is not measured by how flawless it looks. It is measured by how honest it feels.

It feels like: not rushing to say yes just to be liked, to choose rest without guilt, or to speak honestly even if your voice shakes a little

It feels steady, not perfect. It feels lived, not performed. It feels like breathing without holding your breath to present yourself.

You can begin to live a life that feels like you belong inside it. Not because everything is easy, but because you stop treating yourself as something to manage or impress.

The goal is not fearlessness

Some people wait to take action until they feel fearless. They wait to speak until their voice is strong. They wait to try something new until doubt disappears. They wait to set boundaries until guilt goes away. They wait to be seen until they feel impressive. Fearlessness becomes the requirement for living.

> But fearlessness is not the goal. It has never been the goal.

You do not need to be fearless to live honestly. You do not need to eliminate doubt to make aligned choices. Fear can stay in the room without leading the conversation.

In a trustworthy life, fear loses its authority, not its existence. It becomes a signal, not a dictator. It says, "Be careful," not, "Do not live." It says, "Think about this," not, "Hide yourself." It warns, but it does not command.

You can let fear exist like a nervous relative who visits often, but does not get to rearrange your furniture every time they show up.

You do not need fearlessness. You need relationship with yourself. You need to care more about honoring your values than avoiding discomfort. You need to treat fear as a voice, not a verdict.

A trustworthy life still contains fear. But you choose yourself anyway.

Authenticity rewards you in ways perfection never can

When you choose to show up as you are, something subtle begins to shift. The world does not magically become easier. People do not suddenly understand you perfectly. But life begins to feel real. Relationships begin to feel grounded. Creativity becomes more meaningful. Work becomes more human. Rest becomes more deserved.

When you stop performing, you allow yourself to connect.

Perfectionism pushes connection away. Authenticity invites it. Not because people necessarily approve more, but because you begin to feel that you are worth knowing. When you are honest, you no longer worry about being loved for the wrong reasons. You do not have to hide or pretend. You do not have to impress or manage perceptions. You simply have to be real.

And being real strengthens you. It gives you inner stability. It gives you the ability to make choices based on what matters to you, not what would make you appear admirable. It allows you to care for yourself without apology. It allows you to try things even when they might go poorly. It allows you to shape a life based on alignment instead of fear.

Authenticity is not a performance of being different. Authenticity is the absence of pretending. And when you stop pretending, you can finally build a life that supports who you actually are.

A personal blueprint for ongoing growth

You do not need a strict set of steps to live from self trust. Growth is not a checklist. It is a relationship with yourself, and relationships are ongoing. They deepen with attention. They strengthen with caregiving. They remain flexible because you will change as you live.

Here is a simple blueprint you can return to again and again. Not as rules. As reminders.

1. Listen

Listen for the difference between fear and values.

Listen to your body when it is tired.

Listen to your boundaries before they break.

Listen to your creativity before you judge it.

Listen to what you need, not just what you should do.

2. Question

When the critic appears, ask what it is afraid of.

Ask what value it is trying to protect.

Ask whether its warning still applies to your current life.

Ask whether the voice comes from old rules that no longer fit.

3. Choose

Choose what aligns with your values, not with your fear.

Choose rest when your body asks for it.

Choose honesty even if messy.

Choose creativity even if unfinished.

Choose boundaries even if awkward.

4. Follow through

Honor small promises.

Allow yourself to keep showing up, imperfectly.

Let consistency matter more than performance.

Treat yourself like someone worth respecting.

A blueprint is not a command. It is a direction you keep returning to. You will not always follow it perfectly. That is not failure. Growth is not measured by how perfectly you act, but by how kindly you return to yourself when you do not.

Keep listening to your own voice

Your voice is something you will learn over time. It will not always sound confident. It will not always be easy to hear. But it is worth waiting for. Worth listening to. Worth respecting.

As you keep choosing yourself, your voice will grow less afraid. As you keep caring for yourself, your voice will become steadier, and as you keep honoring your needs, honesty will begin to feel natural.

Self trust is not something you achieve once. It is something you keep building, like a relationship with someone you love. You do not need to earn your own respect. You only need to stop abandoning yourself.

Let your inner voice grow with experience. Let it change as you change. Let it mature as you mature. Let it guide you, even when it whispers instead of shouts.

You will not do this perfectly. You are not meant to. Self trust is built through presence, not control.

Workbook Prompts for Chapter Eight

1 Describe what a life guided by self trust looks and feels like.
Focus on how it feels inside you. Not on achievements or

appearances. Describe the tone of your life, the emotional quality, the way you treat yourself.

2 Write down three decisions you will make differently from now on. Small decisions. Sustainable choices. Reflect values, not perfection. Examples might include:

- I will rest without permission from others.
- I will listen to what I need before I say yes.
- I will create even if my work is rough and incomplete.

3 Create a short set of values to live by that feels true to you, not impressive to others. Think about who you want to be for yourself, not for attention. Your values may sound simple or ordinary. That is good. Let them be human. Let them be lived.

You have lived many years trying to manage how you are seen, trying to meet expectations, trying to protect yourself from rejection or judgment. Now you have the chance to live from something much deeper. You can build a life that does not demand perfection, performance, or fearlessness. You can build a life that chooses you back.

A trustworthy life will not always feel easy. But it will feel honest. It will feel human. It will feel like you are no longer working against yourself but walking with yourself. You can choose one small decision at a time. You can return to yourself again and again. You can build a life that supports who you are instead of who you think you need to be.

You do not need permission to live this way. You do not need certainty. You do not need perfection. You only need to treat yourself with the respect you have always deserved.

Trust Yourself Anyway

Take your life and shape it gently.
Choose yourself in small ways.

Let your voice matter to you. Let your values guide you. Let your honesty live in the light.

You can build a life that rewards authenticity. You can build a life that feels steady inside your own skin. You can build a life you can trust yourself in, one real choice at a time.

A Note from the Author

Thank you for spending this time with yourself, and with these pages. If any part of this book helped you choose honesty, rest, curiosity, or courage in even a small way, then you already know what self trust feels like.

May you keep showing up for your life gently, without waiting to be perfect first. May you grow at your own pace. May your choices reflect who you are, not who you think you should be.

You do not owe the world a performance. You owe yourself a relationship you can live with. If that relationship is kind, everything else can become simpler.

I am grateful to have shared this space with you.

    Ella M Bennet

A Note from the Author

A Poem for the Life You Choose
May you grow
not into perfection
but into yourself.

May you listen gently
to your own voice,
even when it trembles.

May your choices be small
but honest,
like seeds that do not need applause
to become a garden.

May you rest when tired,
speak when it matters,
and show up
before you feel ready to impress.

May you trust yourself
not because you know the way,
but because you will walk
with yourself as you go.

www.ingramcontent.com/pod-product-compliance
Lightning Source LLC
Chambersburg PA
CBHW051422070526
44584CB00023B/3535